The Bucket List
Journal for Couples

Copyright © 2012 LoveBook™ LLC
Cover and Internal Design © 2012 LoveBook™ LLC
Design & Illustration by Kim Chapman
Printed in the USA
First Edition

Published by Neuron Publishing
www.neuronpublishing.com
www.LoveBookOnline.com

Our Goals

Written By:

_____

and

_____

Started On:

_____

Table of Contents

Using This Book

Why?

The purpose of this book is to help you, as a couple, come up with a list of goals that you'd like to achieve together. Writing them down not only helps to clarify your individual priorities but also increases the likelihood that you will put your goals into action and make them a reality.

How?

Take a moment to flip through the book. You'll notice that it is broken up into seven main categories.

| Travel | Adventure | Career & Finance | Relationships | Personal Development | Community | Misc. |

The task of trying to come up with all of your life long goals can be overwhelming. Using these categories will help you narrow down your thoughts and focus your ideas.

 We've also included some starter ideas in each section to give you a little inspiration along the way. Just look for the light bulb if you'd like some suggestions.

There's plenty of space to write down all of your goals, as well as a target date for any time sensitive goals, and of course a box for that satisfying check mark after you've completed them!

But don't stop there! Each section also contains a follow up area where you can write about all of your fantastic adventures so that you'll never forget the details of your achievements.

So go ahead, get started! Have a great time learning about each other and planning the amazing journey that lies ahead.

Getting Started

Below are some questions to get those creative juices flowing. Each person should answer them separately. Then compare your answers to see how your future goals are similar and where they differ. This will help you when it comes to deciding on your list of things to do together.

1. As a child, what was something you always dreamt of doing when you grew up?

2. If you had a class reunion coming up, what would you like to be able to tell your classmates that you've done?

3. Who do you most admire? Why?

4. What would you do if you just won the lottery?

5. If you were listening to your own eulogy what would you want to hear someone say about you?

6. What would you do if you had unlimited time and resources?

7. If you could meet anyone living or dead, who would it be? Why?

8. What new activity or skill have you always wanted to try/learn?

9. What have been the most memorable moments in your life so far? Why?

10. What do you want to accomplish in order to look back on your life with no regrets?

"Twenty years from now you
will be more disappointed by the
things you didn't do than by the ones
you did do. So throw off the bowlines,
sail away from the safe harbor. Catch
the trade winds in your sails. Explore.
Dream. Discover."

— Mark Twain

Travel

There's no better way to see the world than with someone special by your side. Wake up on a remote, tropical island, glide along in a gondola in Venice, or take in the sights from the top of a moonlit Eiffel Tower. There are countless destinations waiting to be explored so make your list, pack your bags and head out the door!

> Visit all seven continents, the Great Wall of China, Vatican City, Budapest, the Seven Wonders of the Modern World, the Pyramids, your ancestors' homeland, Niagara Falls, Bora Bora, the Eiffel Tower, take a Mediterranean Cruise or a cross country road trip, see Shanghai, the Wailing Wall, the Taj Mahal, all the Major League baseball stadiums in the U.S., the Himalayas, Seychelles, Venice, Maui, St. Lucia or the Parthanon.

	Goal	Target Date	Done!
1.	_____	_____	☐
2.	_____	_____	☐
3.	_____	_____	☐
4.	_____	_____	☐
5.	_____	_____	☐

Travel

	Goal	Target Date	Done!
6.			☐
7.			☐
8.			☐
9.			☐
10.			☐
11.			☐
12.			☐
13.			☐
14.			☐
15.			☐

Travel

	Goal	Target Date	Done!
16.			☐
17.			☐
18.			☐
19.			☐
20.			☐
21.			☐
22.			☐
23.			☐
24.			☐
25.			☐

Travel

Date we achieved the goal: _____

Which goal we achieved: _____
_____
_____

Where we achieved it: _____
_____

How we achieved it: _____
_____
_____

How we felt: _____
_____
_____

Comments & Anecdotes: _____
_____
_____
_____
_____

Travel

Date we achieved the goal: _____

Which goal we achieved: _____
_____
_____

Where we achieved it: _____
_____

How we achieved it: _____
_____
_____

How we felt: _____
_____
_____

Comments & Anecdotes: _____
_____
_____
_____
_____

Travel

Date we achieved the goal: _____

Which goal we achieved: _____

_____

_____

Where we achieved it: _____

_____

How we achieved it: _____

_____

_____

How we felt: _____

_____

_____

Comments & Anecdotes: _____

_____

_____

_____

_____

_____

Travel

Date we achieved the goal: _____

Which goal we achieved: _____
_____
_____

Where we achieved it: _____
_____

How we achieved it: _____
_____
_____

How we felt: _____
_____
_____

Comments & Anecdotes: _____
_____
_____
_____
_____

Travel

Date we achieved the goal: _____

Which goal we achieved: _____
_____
_____

Where we achieved it: _____
_____

How we achieved it: _____
_____
_____

How we felt: _____
_____
_____

Comments & Anecdotes: _____
_____
_____
_____
_____

Travel

Date we achieved the goal: _____

Which goal we achieved: _____

_____

_____

Where we achieved it: _____

_____

How we achieved it: _____

_____

_____

How we felt: _____

_____

_____

Comments & Anecdotes: _____

_____

_____

_____

_____

_____

13

Travel

Date we achieved the goal: _____

Which goal we achieved: _____
_____
_____

Where we achieved it: _____
_____

How we achieved it: _____
_____
_____

How we felt: _____
_____
_____

Comments & Anecdotes: _____
_____
_____
_____
_____

Travel

Date we achieved the goal: _____

Which goal we achieved: _____
_____
_____

Where we achieved it: _____
_____

How we achieved it: _____
_____
_____

How we felt: _____
_____
_____

Comments & Anecdotes: _____
_____
_____
_____
_____

Travel

Date we achieved the goal: _____

Which goal we achieved: _____

_____

_____

Where we achieved it: _____

_____

How we achieved it: _____

_____

_____

How we felt: _____

_____

_____

Comments & Anecdotes: _____

_____

_____

_____

_____

Travel

Date we achieved the goal: _____

Which goal we achieved: _____
_____
_____

Where we achieved it: _____
_____

How we achieved it: _____
_____
_____

How we felt: _____
_____
_____

Comments & Anecdotes: _____
_____
_____
_____
_____

"We should come home from far,
from adventures, and perils, and
discoveries every day, with new
experience and character."
—Henry David Thoreau

Adventure

Take a risk with someone whom you know has your back. Adrenaline junkies might try hang gliding over the mountains of Patagonia, while newer adventurists might get their feet wet kayaking down a winding river. There's something exhilarating about stepping outside your comfort zone, getting that rush and taking pride in the fact that together you can tackle anything!

> Go skydiving, scuba dive, bungee jump, run with the bulls, base jump, kayak, go white water rafting, learn to surf, parasail, ride a mechanical bull, sail around the world, go hang gliding, take a hot air balloon ride, swim with sharks, drive a race car, climb a mountain, sing karaoke, be part of a flash mob, ring in New Years in Times Square, crowd surf at a concert, ride a horse, fly a helicopter, travel to space, or go cliff diving.

	Goal	Target Date	Done!
1.	_____	_____	☐
2.	_____	_____	☐
3.	_____	_____	☐
4.	_____	_____	☐
5.	_____	_____	☐

Adventure

	Goal	Target Date	Done!
6.			☐
7.			☐
8.			☐
9.			☐
10.			☐
11.			☐
12.			☐
13.			☐
14.			☐
15.			☐

Adventure

	Goal	Target Date	Done!
16.			☐
17.			☐
18.			☐
19.			☐
20.			☐
21.			☐
22.			☐
23.			☐
24.			☐
25.			☐

Adventure

Date we achieved the goal: _____

Which goal we achieved: _____

_____

_____

Where we achieved it: _____

_____

How we achieved it: _____

_____

_____

How we felt: _____

_____

_____

Comments & Anecdotes: _____

_____

_____

_____

_____

Adventure

Date we achieved the goal: _____

Which goal we achieved: _____

_____

_____

Where we achieved it: _____

_____

How we achieved it: _____

_____

_____

How we felt: _____

_____

_____

Comments & Anecdotes: _____

_____

_____

_____

_____

23

Adventure

Date we achieved the goal: _____

Which goal we achieved: _____
_____
_____

Where we achieved it: _____
_____

How we achieved it: _____
_____
_____

How we felt: _____
_____
_____

Comments & Anecdotes: _____
_____
_____
_____
_____

Adventure

Date we achieved the goal: _____

Which goal we achieved: _____
_____
_____

Where we achieved it: _____
_____

How we achieved it: _____
_____
_____

How we felt: _____
_____
_____

Comments & Anecdotes: _____
_____
_____
_____
_____
_____

Adventure

Date we achieved the goal: _____

Which goal we achieved: _____
_____
_____

Where we achieved it: _____
_____

How we achieved it: _____
_____
_____

How we felt: _____
_____
_____

Comments & Anecdotes: _____
_____
_____
_____
_____

Adventure

Date we achieved the goal: _____

Which goal we achieved: _____

_____

_____

Where we achieved it: _____

_____

How we achieved it: _____

_____

_____

How we felt: _____

_____

_____

Comments & Anecdotes: _____

_____

_____

_____

_____

_____

Adventure

Date we achieved the goal: _____

Which goal we achieved: _____
_____
_____

Where we achieved it: _____
_____

How we achieved it: _____
_____
_____

How we felt: _____
_____
_____

Comments & Anecdotes: _____
_____
_____
_____
_____

Adventure

Date we achieved the goal: _____

Which goal we achieved: _____

_____

_____

Where we achieved it: _____

_____

How we achieved it: _____

_____

_____

How we felt: _____

_____

_____

Comments & Anecdotes: _____

_____

_____

_____

_____

Adventure

Date we achieved the goal: _____

Which goal we achieved: _____
_____
_____

Where we achieved it: _____
_____

How we achieved it: _____
_____
_____

How we felt: _____
_____
_____

Comments & Anecdotes: _____
_____
_____
_____
_____
_____

Adventure

Date we achieved the goal: _____

Which goal we achieved: _____

_____

_____

Where we achieved it: _____

_____

How we achieved it: _____

_____

_____

How we felt: _____

_____

_____

Comments & Anecdotes: _____

_____

_____

_____

_____

_____

"Choose a job you love and you will never have to work a day in your life."

— Confucius

"It is never too late to be what you might have been."

— George Eliot

Career & Finance

While career goals may seem more individualistic, ambitions like making partner or going back to school to realize a new dream are much more attainable with the support of a loved one. The same goes for staying on track with a budget or getting out of debt. If you are both working toward the same vision, your odds of success vastly improve.

> Get your dream job, earn a promotion, start your own business, make partner, work internationally, invent something, go back to school, become financially independent, start a 401K, become debt free, own a house, open a savings account, develop a portfolio, save for college, earn your first million, save 6 months of living expenses.

	Goal	Target Date	Done!
1.			☐
2.			☐
3.			☐
4.			☐
5.			☐

Career & Finance

	Goal	Target Date	Done!
6.			☐
7.			☐
8.			☐
9.			☐
10.			☐
11.			☐
12.			☐
13.			☐
14.			☐
15.			☐

Career & Finance

	Goal	Target Date	Done!
16.			☐
17.			☐
18.			☐
19.			☐
20.			☐
21.			☐
22.			☐
23.			☐
24.			☐
25.			☐

Career & Finance

Date we achieved the goal: _____

Which goal we achieved: _____
_____
_____

Where we achieved it: _____
_____

How we achieved it: _____
_____
_____

How we felt: _____
_____
_____

Comments & Anecdotes: _____
_____
_____
_____
_____

Career & Finance

Date we achieved the goal: _____

Which goal we achieved: _____

_____

_____

Where we achieved it: _____

_____

How we achieved it: _____

_____

_____

How we felt: _____

_____

_____

Comments & Anecdotes: _____

_____

_____

_____

_____

Career & Finance

Date we achieved the goal: _____

Which goal we achieved: _____
_____
_____

Where we achieved it: _____
_____

How we achieved it: _____
_____
_____

How we felt: _____
_____
_____

Comments & Anecdotes: _____
_____
_____
_____
_____

Career & Finance

Date we achieved the goal: _____

Which goal we achieved: _____
_____
_____

Where we achieved it: _____
_____

How we achieved it: _____
_____
_____

How we felt: _____
_____
_____

Comments & Anecdotes: _____
_____
_____
_____
_____

Career & Finance

Date we achieved the goal: _____

Which goal we achieved: _____

_____

_____

Where we achieved it: _____

_____

How we achieved it: _____

_____

_____

How we felt: _____

_____

_____

Comments & Anecdotes: _____

_____

_____

_____

_____

_____

Career & Finance

Date we achieved the goal: _____

Which goal we achieved: _____

_____

_____

Where we achieved it: _____

_____

How we achieved it: _____

_____

_____

How we felt: _____

_____

_____

Comments & Anecdotes: _____

_____

_____

_____

_____

Career & Finance

Date we achieved the goal: _____

Which goal we achieved: _____

_____

_____

Where we achieved it: _____

_____

How we achieved it: _____

_____

_____

How we felt: _____

_____

_____

Comments & Anecdotes: _____

_____

_____

_____

_____

Career & Finance

Date we achieved the goal: _____

Which goal we achieved: _____
_____
_____

Where we achieved it: _____
_____

How we achieved it: _____
_____
_____

How we felt: _____
_____
_____

Comments & Anecdotes: _____
_____
_____
_____
_____

Career & Finance

Date we achieved the goal: _____

Which goal we achieved: _____
_____
_____

Where we achieved it: _____
_____

How we achieved it: _____
_____
_____

How we felt: _____
_____
_____

Comments & Anecdotes: _____
_____
_____
_____
_____

Career & Finance

Date we achieved the goal: _____

Which goal we achieved: _____

_____

_____

Where we achieved it: _____

_____

How we achieved it: _____

_____

_____

How we felt: _____

_____

_____

Comments & Anecdotes: _____

_____

_____

_____

_____

_____

"The best and most beautiful
things in the world cannot be seen
or even touched. They must be
felt with the heart."

— Helen Keller

Relationships

Healthy relationships are an essential part of any happy, fulfilled life. Whether its improving communication between the two of you, putting more effort into your friendships or deciding to expand your family, relationship goals can be some of the most challenging to achieve, but they are often the most rewarding.

> Reconnect with a lost friend or family member, retrace your family tree, make a regular date night, have children, organize a reunion, forgive someone who has hurt you, adopt a child, renew your vows, meet your neighbors, apologize to someone who you hurt, throw a surprise party for someone special, record your family's stories/history, host your family for Thanksgiving, spend the whole day in bed, adopt a pet.

	Goal	Target Date	Done!
1.			☐
2.			☐
3.			☐
4.			☐
5.			☐

Relationships

	Goal	Target Date	Done!
6.			☐
7.			☐
8.			☐
9.			☐
10.			☐
11.			☐
12.			☐
13.			☐
14.			☐
15.			☐

Relationships

	Goal	Target Date	Done!
16.			☐
17.			☐
18.			☐
19.			☐
20.			☐
21.			☐
22.			☐
23.			☐
24.			☐
25.			☐

Relationships

Date we achieved the goal: _____

Which goal we achieved: _____
_____
_____

Where we achieved it: _____
_____

How we achieved it: _____
_____
_____

How we felt: _____
_____
_____

Comments & Anecdotes: _____
_____
_____
_____
_____

Relationships

Date we achieved the goal: _____

Which goal we achieved: _____

_____

_____

Where we achieved it: _____

_____

How we achieved it: _____

_____

_____

How we felt: _____

_____

_____

Comments & Anecdotes: _____

_____

_____

_____

_____

_____

Relationships

Date we achieved the goal: _____

Which goal we achieved: _____
_____
_____

Where we achieved it: _____
_____

How we achieved it: _____
_____
_____

How we felt: _____
_____
_____

Comments & Anecdotes: _____
_____
_____
_____
_____

Relationships

Date we achieved the goal: _____

Which goal we achieved: _____

_____

_____

Where we achieved it: _____

_____

How we achieved it: _____

_____

_____

How we felt: _____

_____

_____

Comments & Anecdotes: _____

_____

_____

_____

_____

_____

Relationships

Date we achieved the goal: _____

Which goal we achieved: _____
_____
_____

Where we achieved it: _____
_____

How we achieved it: _____
_____
_____

How we felt: _____
_____
_____

Comments & Anecdotes: _____
_____
_____
_____
_____

Relationships

Date we achieved the goal: _____

Which goal we achieved: _____
_____
_____

Where we achieved it: _____
_____

How we achieved it: _____
_____
_____

How we felt: _____
_____
_____

Comments & Anecdotes: _____
_____
_____
_____
_____

Relationships

Date we achieved the goal: _____

Which goal we achieved: _____
_____
_____

Where we achieved it: _____
_____

How we achieved it: _____
_____
_____

How we felt: _____
_____
_____

Comments & Anecdotes: _____
_____
_____
_____
_____
_____

Relationships

Date we achieved the goal: _____

Which goal we achieved: _____

_____

_____

Where we achieved it: _____

_____

How we achieved it: _____

_____

_____

How we felt: _____

_____

_____

Comments & Anecdotes: _____

_____

_____

_____

_____

_____

Relationships

Date we achieved the goal: _____

Which goal we achieved: _____
_____
_____

Where we achieved it: _____
_____

How we achieved it: _____
_____
_____

How we felt: _____
_____
_____

Comments & Anecdotes: _____
_____
_____
_____
_____

Relationships

Date we achieved the goal: _____

Which goal we achieved: _____

_____

_____

Where we achieved it: _____

_____

How we achieved it: _____

_____

_____

How we felt: _____

_____

_____

Comments & Anecdotes: _____

_____

_____

_____

_____

_____

"Without continual growth
and progress, such words as
improvement, achievement, and
success have no meaning."

— Benjamin Franklin

Personal Development

If you've ever felt stuck in a rut, personal development goals are a great way to expand your horizons. Learn something new, try out a hobby you've always found interesting or commit to kicking a bad habit. Try to stay open minded to your partner's suggestions. You never know, those yoga classes may be a whole lot more beneficial than you first thought.

> Learn a new language, complete a degree, read one book a week for a year, take dance lessons, learn to play an instrument and play a duet, write and publish a book, write a song for each other, make a movie, paint a mural, find a place of worship, meditate, try yoga or pilates, achieve a healthy weight, quit smoking, run a marathon, compete in a triathlon, become vegetarian, learn to play tennis, plant a garden, get tattoos.

	Goal	Target Date	Done!
1.	_____	_____	☐
2.	_____	_____	☐
3.	_____	_____	☐
4.	_____	_____	☐
5.	_____	_____	☐

Personal Development

	Goal	Target Date	Done!
6.			☐
7.			☐
8.			☐
9.			☐
10.			☐
11.			☐
12.			☐
13.			☐
14.			☐
15.			☐

Personal Development

	Goal	Target Date	Done!
16.			☐
17.			☐
18.			☐
19.			☐
20.			☐
21.			☐
22.			☐
23.			☐
24.			☐
25.			☐

Personal Development

Date we achieved the goal: _____

Which goal we achieved: _____
_____
_____

Where we achieved it: _____
_____

How we achieved it: _____
_____
_____

How we felt: _____
_____
_____

Comments & Anecdotes: _____
_____
_____
_____
_____

Personal Development

Date we achieved the goal: _____

Which goal we achieved: _____

_____

_____

Where we achieved it: _____

_____

How we achieved it: _____

_____

_____

How we felt: _____

_____

_____

Comments & Anecdotes: _____

_____

_____

_____

_____

_____

Personal Development

Date we achieved the goal: _____

Which goal we achieved: _____
_____
_____

Where we achieved it: _____
_____

How we achieved it: _____
_____
_____

How we felt: _____
_____
_____

Comments & Anecdotes: _____
_____
_____
_____
_____

Personal Development

Date we achieved the goal: _____

Which goal we achieved: _____

_____

_____

Where we achieved it: _____

_____

How we achieved it: _____

_____

_____

How we felt: _____

_____

_____

Comments & Anecdotes: _____

_____

_____

_____

_____

_____

Personal Development

Date we achieved the goal: _____

Which goal we achieved: _____
_____
_____

Where we achieved it: _____
_____

How we achieved it: _____
_____
_____

How we felt: _____
_____
_____

Comments & Anecdotes: _____
_____
_____
_____
_____
_____

Personal Development

Date we achieved the goal: _____

Which goal we achieved: _____
_____
_____

Where we achieved it: _____
_____

How we achieved it: _____
_____
_____

How we felt: _____
_____
_____

Comments & Anecdotes: _____
_____
_____
_____
_____
_____

Personal Development

Date we achieved the goal: _____

Which goal we achieved: _____
_____
_____

Where we achieved it: _____
_____

How we achieved it: _____
_____
_____

How we felt: _____
_____
_____

Comments & Anecdotes: _____
_____
_____
_____
_____

Personal Development

Date we achieved the goal: _____

Which goal we achieved: _____

_____

_____

Where we achieved it: _____

_____

How we achieved it: _____

_____

_____

How we felt: _____

_____

_____

Comments & Anecdotes: _____

_____

_____

_____

_____

Personal Development

Date we achieved the goal: _____

Which goal we achieved: _____
_____
_____

Where we achieved it: _____
_____

How we achieved it: _____
_____
_____

How we felt: _____
_____
_____

Comments & Anecdotes: _____
_____
_____
_____
_____
_____

Personal Development

Date we achieved the goal: _____

Which goal we achieved: _____
_____
_____

Where we achieved it: _____
_____

How we achieved it: _____
_____
_____

How we felt: _____
_____
_____

Comments & Anecdotes: _____
_____
_____
_____
_____
_____

"I expect to pass through life but once. If therefore, there be any kindness I can show, or any good thing I can do to any fellow being, let me do it now, and not defer or neglect it, as I shall not pass this way again."

— William Penn

Community

There are few things more rewarding in life than the feeling you get from helping someone in need. It doesn't have to be a grand gesture, and no one is expecting you to become Mother Teresa. Start small and take a look around your own neighborhood. Find something that has particular meaning to both of you, roll up your sleeves and get busy.

> Donate your time to a charity, go on a mission trip, help with a city beautification project, visit an elderly neighbor, start a book club, become a Scout leader, donate blood, start a recycling initiate, form a neighborhood watch program, contribute monthly to a charity, volunteer at an animal shelter, organize a food drive, become a mentor to a child, build a school in a developing nation, organize a toy drive for children in need.

	Goal	Target Date	Done!
1.			☐
2.			☐
3.			☐
4.			☐
5.			☐

Community

	Goal	Target Date	Done!
6.			☐
7.			☐
8.			☐
9.			☐
10.			☐
11.			☐
12.			☐
13.			☐
14.			☐
15.			☐

Community

	Goal	Target Date	Done!
16.			☐
17.			☐
18.			☐
19.			☐
20.			☐
21.			☐
22.			☐
23.			☐
24.			☐
25.			☐

Community

Date we achieved the goal: _____

Which goal we achieved: _____
_____
_____

Where we achieved it: _____
_____

How we achieved it: _____
_____
_____

How we felt: _____
_____
_____

Comments & Anecdotes: _____
_____
_____
_____
_____
_____

Community

Date we achieved the goal: _____

Which goal we achieved: _____
_____
_____

Where we achieved it: _____
_____

How we achieved it: _____
_____
_____

How we felt: _____
_____
_____

Comments & Anecdotes: _____
_____
_____
_____
_____
_____

Community

Date we achieved the goal: _____

Which goal we achieved: _____
_____
_____

Where we achieved it: _____
_____

How we achieved it: _____
_____
_____

How we felt: _____
_____
_____

Comments & Anecdotes: _____
_____
_____
_____
_____
_____

Community

Date we achieved the goal: _____

Which goal we achieved: _____

_____

_____

Where we achieved it: _____

_____

How we achieved it: _____

_____

_____

How we felt: _____

_____

_____

Comments & Anecdotes: _____

_____

_____

_____

_____

_____

Community

Date we achieved the goal: _____

Which goal we achieved: _____
_____
_____

Where we achieved it: _____
_____

How we achieved it: _____
_____
_____

How we felt: _____
_____
_____

Comments & Anecdotes: _____
_____
_____
_____
_____

Community

Date we achieved the goal: _____

Which goal we achieved: _____
_____
_____

Where we achieved it: _____
_____

How we achieved it: _____
_____
_____

How we felt: _____
_____
_____

Comments & Anecdotes: _____
_____
_____
_____
_____

Community

Date we achieved the goal: _____

Which goal we achieved: _____
_____
_____

Where we achieved it: _____
_____

How we achieved it: _____
_____
_____

How we felt: _____
_____
_____

Comments & Anecdotes: _____
_____
_____
_____
_____

Community

Date we achieved the goal: _____

Which goal we achieved: _____

_____

_____

Where we achieved it: _____

_____

How we achieved it: _____

_____

_____

How we felt: _____

_____

_____

Comments & Anecdotes: _____

_____

_____

_____

_____

Community

Date we achieved the goal: _____

Which goal we achieved: _____

_____

_____

Where we achieved it: _____

_____

How we achieved it: _____

_____

_____

How we felt: _____

_____

_____

Comments & Anecdotes: _____

_____

_____

_____

_____

_____

Community

Date we achieved the goal: _____

Which goal we achieved: _____

_____

_____

Where we achieved it: _____

_____

How we achieved it: _____

_____

_____

How we felt: _____

_____

_____

Comments & Anecdotes: _____

_____

_____

_____

_____

"You don't have to be a fantastic
hero to do certain things -- to
compete. You can be just an ordinary
chap, sufficiently motivated to
reach challenging goals."
— Sir Edmund Hillary

Miscellaneous

Not every goal that you make will fit neatly in a predefined category. Your dreams should be as unique as the two of you. Go with what moves you, whatever that may be. Conquer a fear, make time to smell the roses or just do something unexpected. There are no right or wrong goals and nothing is off the table so long as you're achieving them together!

> Go through a haunted house, win a tag-team pie eating contest, start your own garage band, learn to whistle, start a new tradition that is just for the two of you, order only new things when you go out to restaurants, play in the rain, climb to the top of a tree, win a couple's costume contest, spend all day in bed, keep a diary together, make a time capsule, see the Olympics in person, tryout drastic new hairstyles.

	Goal	Target Date	Done!
1.			☐
2.			☐
3.			☐
4.			☐
5.			☐

Miscellaneous

	Goal	Target Date	Done!
6.			☐
7.			☐
8.			☐
9.			☐
10.			☐
11.			☐
12.			☐
13.			☐
14.			☐
15.			☐

Miscellaneous

	Goal	Target Date	Done!
16.			☐
17.			☐
18.			☐
19.			☐
20.			☐
21.			☐
22.			☐
23.			☐
24.			☐
25.			☐

Miscellaneous

Date we achieved the goal: _____

Which goal we achieved: _____
_____
_____

Where we achieved it: _____
_____

How we achieved it: _____
_____
_____

How we felt: _____
_____
_____

Comments & Anecdotes: _____
_____
_____
_____
_____
_____

Miscellaneous

Date we achieved the goal: _____

Which goal we achieved: _____

_____

_____

Where we achieved it: _____

_____

How we achieved it: _____

_____

_____

How we felt: _____

_____

_____

Comments & Anecdotes: _____

_____

_____

_____

_____

_____

Miscellaneous

Date we achieved the goal: _____

Which goal we achieved: _____
_____
_____

Where we achieved it: _____
_____

How we achieved it: _____
_____
_____

How we felt: _____
_____
_____

Comments & Anecdotes: _____
_____
_____
_____
_____

Miscellaneous

Date we achieved the goal: _____

Which goal we achieved: _____

_____

_____

Where we achieved it: _____

_____

How we achieved it: _____

_____

_____

How we felt: _____

_____

_____

Comments & Anecdotes: _____

_____

_____

_____

_____

_____

Miscellaneous

Date we achieved the goal: _____

Which goal we achieved: _____
_____
_____

Where we achieved it: _____
_____

How we achieved it: _____
_____
_____

How we felt: _____
_____
_____

Comments & Anecdotes: _____
_____
_____
_____
_____
_____

Miscellaneous

Date we achieved the goal: _____

Which goal we achieved: _____
_____
_____

Where we achieved it: _____
_____

How we achieved it: _____
_____
_____

How we felt: _____
_____
_____

Comments & Anecdotes: _____
_____
_____
_____
_____
_____

Miscellaneous

Date we achieved the goal: _____

Which goal we achieved: _____

_____

_____

Where we achieved it: _____

_____

How we achieved it: _____

_____

_____

How we felt: _____

_____

_____

Comments & Anecdotes: _____

_____

_____

_____

_____

_____

Miscellaneous

Date we achieved the goal: _____

Which goal we achieved: _____
_____
_____

Where we achieved it: _____
_____

How we achieved it: _____
_____
_____

How we felt: _____
_____
_____

Comments & Anecdotes: _____
_____
_____
_____
_____

Miscellaneous

Date we achieved the goal: _____

Which goal we achieved: _____
_____
_____

Where we achieved it: _____
_____

How we achieved it: _____
_____
_____

How we felt: _____
_____
_____

Comments & Anecdotes: _____
_____
_____
_____
_____

Miscellaneous

Date we achieved the goal: _____

Which goal we achieved: _____
_____
_____

Where we achieved it: _____
_____

How we achieved it: _____
_____
_____

How we felt: _____
_____
_____

Comments & Anecdotes: _____
_____
_____
_____
_____
_____

Other LoveBook™ Titles

The Original "LoveBook™"

A LoveBook™ is a personalized book that you create with all the reasons why you love that special someone. It's fun, easy and makes a great gift for any of your loved ones.

The Activity Book for Couples

Whether you are just dating or have been together for 50 years, these fun games and drawing activities are sure to bring laughter to your day!

The Romantic Coupon Book

A fun, romantic coupon book for anyone in love. These humorous discounts and freebies will keep your partner occupied for months! Contains 22 illustrated coupons.

The Marriage Advice Journal

This makes a great wedding or shower gift. Put all of the words of wisdom from friends and family on how to make the most of a marriage in one convenient book.

The Quiz Book for Couples

Think you know everything about your significant other? Put your knowledge to the test with this fun book of questions for every aspect of your relationship.

Let's Get Naked: The Sexy Activity Book for Couples

Need to spice up your sex life? This book has games, quizzes, challenges and other fun stuff to get you & your partner in the mood for a little bump and tickle!

Spread The Love

This book lists 75 simple ways to make a significant impact on the lives around you. The ideas are easily categorized by: Acts of Service, Quality Time, Giving, Physical Support, and Communication. Choose to make a positive difference by spreading the love today.

Try Something New

Even the most adventurous couples can find themselves in a rut from time to time. With 100 fun and creative ways to shake things up, this book will challenge you to get outside of your usual activities.

All of these titles and more can be found at www.LoveBookOnline.com

About LoveBook™

We are a group of individuals who want to spread love in all it's forms. We believe love fuels the world and every relationship is important. We hope this book helps build on that belief.

CPSIA information can be obtained at www.ICGtesting.com
Printed in the USA
BVOW07s0628060214

344020BV00001B/130/P